Mastery
of
Self

Mastery
of
Self

CHRISTIAN DAA LARSON

NEW YORK

Mastery of Self
Cover © 2007 Cosimo, Inc.

For information, address:

Cosimo, P.O. Box 416
Old Chelsea Station
New York, NY 10113-0416

or visit our website at:
www.cosimobooks.com

Mastery of Self was originally published in 1907.

Cover design by www.kerndesign.net

ISBN: 978-1-60206-176-7

He who is willing to lose the smaller life
for the sake of the larger, will gain the larger;
and he who is willing to lose his limited personal power
for the sake of unlimited impersonal power,
will gain the unlimited.

——from *Mastery of Self*

Mastery of Self

MAN is made, for attainment and achievement; to ever become greater and greater than he is now—that is the purpose of his life; and to promote that purpose he must ever advance in the mastery of self. To move forward in the path of attainment, everything in the being of man must be employed constructively; every process in mind or body must become a building process, and all the elements and forces in the human system must work together towards the great goal in view; but to direct the whole of self to work for a greater self demands the mastery of self.

No power in man can do what it is created to do, and what it has the capacity to do, until it is directed by man himself; powers, elements, forces, and things are at the disposal of man; they can do only what he directs them to do; they respond only to his control, but before man can gain the power to master forces and things, he must gain the power to master himself.

When man has gained the power to control himself he can control everything in his world without trying to control anything. It is therefore evident that he who is trying to control everything has not learned how to control anything. The true master never tries to master anything, not even himself. He does not have to try to be a master—he is a master.

Nor is it necessary to try to be a master in order to reach that state where one is a master; in fact, no person can learn to control himself so long as he tries to control himself.

To eliminate every desire to master oneself is the first step towards the attainment of the mastery of self. He who does not wish to control anything is alone prepared to gain the power to control everything.

He who tries to control himself, or who tries to control anything that exists outside of himself gives everything in his being the tendency to work towards the surface; the power that produces the mastery of self, however, can only be gained by training the mind to move in the opposite direction.

To master self is to have the power to produce any effect desired in any part of mind or body, and to produce any effect desired it is necessary to produce the corre-sponding cause; but to produce any cause the mind must act in the world of cause—

a world which exists, not on the surface of thought or being, but in the great within.

The harder one tries to control himself the nearer to the surface will the mind act, and the further will mental action be separated from that interior mental state from which one may gain the power to control himself.

He who tries to attain the mastery of self will act entirely upon the outer mental world of effect, and will therefore be unable to create the cause that can produce the mastery of self. The mind must act back of, beneath and above the effect in order to change or produce the cause.

The state of self-mastery is an effect; it is the result of certain attainments; therefore, to produce the state of self-mastery, one must not act upon the state of self-mastery, but must proceed to promote those attainments that naturally result in self-mastery.

It is not possible, however, to promote these attainments while the mind is trying to exercise control over things; to try to control things is to think about things and act directly upon things, and no mind that is acting upon things can act upon the power that controls things.

Each power in the being of man will, when expressed, do the very thing that it is naturally adapted for; that is, it will produce its own natural effect; therefore, to secure any desired effect, the secret is to awaken that power that will, of itself, produce that effect.

However, to awaken any power in the being of man, the mind must act directly upon that state where the power originates; and every power in man originates in the great within.

There is an inner source of everything that appears in the human personality, and to master self is to have the power to cause this inner source to bring forth into the personal self whatever we desire to have expressed through the self.

What the self is to be, and to do, is determined by what is expressed through the self; therefore, when we can cause the inner source to bring forth into the self whatever we may desire, the self will be and do whatever we may desire. And when we can cause the self to be what we wish it to be, and do what we wish it to do, at any time and under any circumstance, then it is that we have gained the mastery of self.

THE mastery of self is an attainment that has no end. Though everything in mind and body may be mastered to-day, to-morrow will bring forth from the great within new forces, new talents, new powers, and new fields of consciousness, all of which demand control and direction if they are to serve their purpose and be of the greatest possible use to man.

Everything that exists in the being of man is created for some purpose, and the whole of life is not lived as it is intended to be lived unless every such purpose is fulfilled; but nothing in man can fulfil its purpose unless it is mastered by the ruling power in man.

The attainment of self-mastery is therefore indispensable to the living of life, and the promotion of the greatest welfare of the whole of life.

Those elements, forces, faculties, talents, and functions that are only partially under control do not serve the life of man as extensively as they might; in fact, many of these, even those that we have been conscious of for ages, serve us but little; and the cause is deficiency in the art of self-mastery.

There are only a few minds that accomplish as much with their talents as it is possible to accomplish at present; the majority, even among the most gifted, seldom use their ability in its full capacity because they have only a limited control over that ability.

That person who has perfect control of himself can accomplish from two to five times as much with a given talent as those who have no more self-control than is found among the average.

To those who seek to attain much and achieve much, self-mastery is therefore invaluable, though it is equally important in the minor affairs of every-day life; a fact that will readily be admitted when we realize how much distress comes hourly to millions because they cannot control their feelings, emotions, thoughts, and actions.

A large share of the mistakes that are made every moment, can be traced directly to a lack of self-control; and the same can be said of sickness, trouble and failure. To have health, happiness and harmony, peace, power and plenty, self-mastery, to a high degree, is necessary; in brief, the only life that is worth while is the life that is lived in the mastery of self.

To attain the mastery of self, it is first necessary to establish firmly in mind the fundamental purpose of mastery. This is extremely important, because to proceed with the wrong purpose in view is to make every effort useless. This, however, is what has been done by nearly everyone who has undertaken the attainment of self-mastery; and nearly all the books that have been written on the subject have been based upon the wrong purpose; they have therefore retarded the very thing which they aimed to promote.

This being true, it is simple to understand why it is practically impossible to find a single person who has attained complete mastery over self.

Nearly every system purporting to teach the art of self-mastery has been based upon the purpose of controlling something, or exercising arbitrary rulership over mind, body, circumstances, and things. But so long as the mind is trying to control something, the power that can control that something will not be gained.

We must remember, at the very beginning, that before the power of self-mastery can be developed and the state of complete mastery attained, all desire to exercise control over anything or anybody must be eliminated absolutely.

The purpose of self-mastery is to give the mind the power to make the fullest and the most perfect use of all the gifts that one may possess now; to be one's best in every sense of the term, at all times, and under all circumstances; to fulfil the purpose of life thoroughly during every passing moment; to live a larger life, a better life, and a more beautiful life every day; to be all that one can be now, and to do all that one can do now; to bring forth continually the very best that may exist in the great within, and to use that best in such a way that the very best will always come to pass.

The true purpose of self-mastery is to make yourself more perfect, more competent, and more useful. In other words, to become much and accomplish much, in order that you may not only be your complete self, but also be an inspiration to all those who believe in the new race, the superior race, the race of mental mastery and soul supremacy.

T HE problem of causing everything in life to become right will easily be solved when man becomes great enough to produce only that which is right; and this greatness will inevitably come when the mastery of self is attained.

That man may become infinitely more than he is now, and that he can do far greater things than has ever been done before, we know with a certainty; we also know that it is the purpose of human life to go on to greatness and greater greatness, but every step must be preceded by another degree in the mastery of self.

When we understand life we invariably gain a strong desire to develop superiority; first, because it is right to attain superiority, and second, because we may thereby inspire thousands to press on to those same magnificent heights.

We desire to demonstrate superiority, however, not for the sake of applause, but to prove by example what man can do. We seek greatness, not that we may rule over anything or anybody, but that we may fulfil the law of life which declares that man is created to become greater and greater so long as eternity shall continue to be.

Our object is not to control those things that exist about us, but to develop those things that exist within us. We seek the fulness of life, and the power to be of the greatest possible use in life; and we seek self-mastery because through mastery alone can these things be promoted to the very highest degree.

When the true purpose of self-mastery is firmly established in mind, we may proceed to develop the power that does produce self-mastery; but the true purpose must never be ignored, because growth in mastery will awaken new forces, new states of consciousness, and new possibilities, and these must all be properly directed.

The higher the power the stronger its force; therefore, the higher we go in the scale of attainment the more important it becomes to properly direct everything.

The misdirection of the higher forces will not only produce all manner of ills, troubles, and failures, but will produce mental phenomena that is misleading. The understanding of truth or any phase of truth will thereby become extremely difficult; in fact, it will be practically impossible to know the real truth about anything so long as such misdirections prevail.

To avoid absolutely the misdirection of any power, fix attention upon development; seek the mastery of self and everything that exists in yourself because you desire to promote greatness in yourself, and you will continue to remain on the right path.

When every thought is animated with a strong desire for a more perfect body, a larger mind, and a more beautiful soul, every effort towards the attainment of self-mastery will become constructive, and only good results can possibly follow.

The less you think about the outer self, and the more you think about the inner self, the better, because it is through the perfect expression of the inner self that you will gain the power to master the outer self.

To clearly, firmly, and permanently establish in mind what one desires to master is extremely important; also, what self-control will mean when it is attained, and what will happen to mind and body when the power of mastery is exercised.

There is a current belief among many that to master oneself is to have the power to interfere with natural functions at will; to suspend the action of this or that organ without producing serious results, and to violate natural laws without having to undergo any of the natural consequences. Others believe that mastery consists in the forceful control of anything and everything that may exist in one's system or in one's circumstances; but such conclusions are the very opposites to the truth.

The majority, however, entertain those very ideas concerning self-mastery; and this is one of the principal reasons why their efforts to attain self-mastery cannot possibly succeed.

He who has attained the mastery of self never tries to suspend the action of any organ; he never thinks of interfering with natural functions in any way whatever, nor does he ignore or violate a single natural law. He never tries to control anything or anybody, not even himself. In fact, the desire to control has been eliminated completely from his mind. His object is not to control himself, but to make the best possible use of himself; and to try to exercise control over something is to interfere with the best use of that something.

The greatest use of self comes directly from the greatest mastery of self, but it is not possible to attain the greatest mastery of self unless the greatest use of self is made the one sole purpose in view.

He who has no desire to control anything, but is inspired with a strong, irresistible desire to make the greatest use of everything, has entered the path to the mastery of self. Without trying to control anything, everything will naturally and willingly come under his control, and will do whatsoever he may wish to have done.

TO master oneself means to direct all the elements, forces, functions, and faculties in the system for the purpose of promoting their natural activities to the highest degree of perfection.

To master one's desires does not mean to suspend those desires, but to give those desires more life and power than ever before, and then direct them into channels of action where the greatest and best results can be obtained under present circumstances.

When you have a desire to do a certain thing and the force of that desire is at hand in the system ready to act, but present circumstances will not permit the expression of that desire, instead of suspending that desire, thereby wasting the energy that was ready for action, you simply turn the force of that desire into some other channel. In this way, valuable results may be secured from the force of every desire that appears in the system, whether the original impulse of that desire can be carried out or not.

Whenever a desire is crushed or suspended all the energy that was alive in that desire will be wasted; and the same waste takes place when a desire is carried in the system

B

for hours, days or weeks, to wear itself out, so to speak, without having its active power turned into any channel of constructive action.

To feel a desire is simply to feel the presence of energy; a desire conveys to the mind the fact that there is energy in the system ready to do something; and if this energy is not given the opportunity to do something it will be wasted.

Through the attainment of self-mastery all the energy that comes into action in the system can be turned into any channel of constructive expression that may be convenient at the time; in fact, to master a desire does not mean to suspend that desire so that it is not felt any more, but to change the course of the force that is active in that desire, so that something of value may be accomplished now while that force is in working condition.

The master-mind never destroys a single desire; he not even thinks of putting down a single feeling that may arise in the system; when he cannot carry out the original desire, or when he finds that the original desire is not normal, which is frequently the case, he redirects the forces that are felt in the system causing them to do something else, something that is normal, and that is possible now.

To master the natural functions is not to

interfere with the purpose of those functions, but to promote that purpose to the very highest degree of perfection.

You can master a natural function when you can cause that function to perform its work perfectly under all sorts of conditions, and thereafter, to continue to further perfect the perfection of its perfect work.

To master the organs and functions of digestion does not mean that you can cause those organs to digest anything that you might take into the system; self-mastery does not violate law, neither does it wilfully admit an enemy in order that it may demonstrate its power to overcome that enemy. Self-mastery does not resist what is not wanted, but gives man the power to create and secure that which is wanted.

To master the organs of digestion would mean to keep those organs continually in such a perfect state of action that whatever the system needs could be digested perfectly, and without the slightest unpleasant sensation at any time or under any circumstance.

To master the heart does not mean that you can increase or decrease the heart-beats at will, but that you can keep the heart constantly in its true, normal action, no matter how much confusion or excitement there may be in your immediate environment.

The attainment of mastery, therefore, does not mean to interfere with natural action, but to promote natural action to the highest possible degree of perfection.

The idea of mastery is perfect action of all things at all times, regardless of circumstances or events. When you attain self-mastery, all things in your system will be doing their work perfectly, at all times, no matter what your work or your environment may be. And, in addition, this perfect action will constantly develop higher degrees of perfect action.

To master the elements and the forces of the system is not only to promote normal action in the chemical world, but to increase the quality and the power of that action by producing new and superior compounds.

Every mind forms different compounds, unconsciously, as the various grades of vibration are entered by the predominating mental states; but what is formed unconsciously is not always desirable, and when it is desirable it is always inferior to what might have been produced through a similar, intelligently directed conscious action.

Mental states of anger usually produce poisonous elements in the system, while states of fear and depression convert healthy tissues into useless, foreign matter. Such matter always clogs the system, thus interfering with natural functions, and producing, directly or indirectly, a number of ills.

Mental states that are lofty, true, and constructive produce chemical compounds in the system that are nourishing and vitalizing, and that have a strong, refining tendency.

Through the power of self-mastery, undesirable compounds may be prevented entirely because the mind that masters self will not create other than wholesome mental states. Through the same power we may so direct and blend the elements of the system that the formation of the most beneficial and the most highly refined compounds may be constantly taking place.

The possibilities of this law are marvellous to say the least; it is through this law that false chemical conditions in the system may be transformed instantaneously into normal and wholesome actions, and it is through this law that all the elements of the physical body may be constantly refined, until absolute regeneration and spiritualization has taken place.

Through this law the physical body can be developed to the very highest degree of purity, wholeness, refinement, and perfection, and made as beautiful as the Ideal Form itself. The application of this law, however, is possible only to those who have attained the mastery of self.

TO master the forces of the system, the principal object in view is to gain power to accumulate those forces in any part of mind or body where important work is to be done now; because, by giving all the power at hand now to the work we are doing now, that work will invariably result in a superior product.

To employ this method at all times would not only cause all things to be done well, but all things would constantly be done better, and failure would be a thing of the past.

If we would give the greater part of our active energy to the organs of digestion during meals, and for a short time after meals, we should never have anything but the most perfect digestion.

If we would give all the forces of intelligence and genius to the faculty that is in action now, that faculty would invariably do the work of genius, and would never fail to improve upon its own previous record.

The possibilities of self-mastery as applied to the forces of the system are therefore extraordinary; but we cannot master the forces of the system by trying to control those forces; to master any force, the will must act, not upon the force itself, but upon the interior cause of that force.

In the mastery of faculties, the purpose must be expansion and enlargement of conscious action; the average mind needs expansion of consciousness because most of its faculties are too small to give expression to all the energy of the system when concentration and accumulation take place. When this expansion has begun, however, quality, efficiency, and volume may always be secured through the action of any faculty or talent.

Consequently, in the mental world one of the principal objects of self-mastery will be to lead consciousness into the realization of new and greater realms of perception and illumination, and to awaken a greater and greater measure of the great within.

The first real step in the mastery of self is to eliminate all desire to control what is exterior to yourself. Train your mind to desire only the mastery of your own being, and refuse absolutely to even think of controlling anything else. We cannot possibly master ourselves so long as there is the slightest desire to control others.

This may seem to be a contradiction of terms, because when one is master, he ought to be master of everything, whether it be in the without or in the within. But though mastery implies the mastery of everything, the fact must not be forgotten that the mastery of the without is simply an effect of the mastery of the within.

The mastery of environments, circum-stances, and external things, naturally follows when one has mastered himself; but so long as we try to control external things we can-not control ourselves, because we cannot produce causes while trying to interfere with effects.

The mastery of self can only be attained through the control of the inner side of mind, consciousness, thought, and action; and to control the inner side constantly, the whole of attention must constantly be given to the inner side.

You control the exterior by causing the interior to become exactly what you wish the exterior to be.

The principle is, produce the cause you want and you will have the effect you want. The cause can be produced only by acting upon the subjective, because it is only the subjective side that has the power to originate cause; and to act upon the subjective, the forces of the mind must be trained to move towards the within.

However, whenever we try to control that which is exterior to ourselves, the forces of the mind will begin to move towards the without; and it is not possible for the forces of mind to go in while they are going out, neither can the tendency to act upon the within be established in mind so long as the outward movement of mind is permitted in the least.

The mind of the average person has already a strong tendency to move towards the surface ; therefore, to remove that tendency completely, the opposite tendency must be given the whole of attention ; all the forces of mind must move towards the within at all times, and attention must be concentrated upon the subjective side absolutely without any cessation whatever.

It is not possible to form a tendency towards the inner life while the mind is acting more or less upon external things ; a tendency is a continuous movement in a certain direction; therefore, while the mind is acting more or less upon the surface, the continuous movement towards the within will be interrupted and there will be no tendency towards the within.

We cannot train mental tendencies to move in opposite directions ; no two forces, directly opposed to each other, can exist in the mind at the same time.

If the entire mind is to be harmonious and constructive, all the forces of the mind must move towards the within ; that is, they must move into the mind and not out of the mind. The person, however, who is trying to control external things while he is trying to develop the mastery of self, will cause his mind to be divided against itself. He will consequently control nothing.

When we realize the difference between the control of self and the control of others, and how they are direct opposites in purpose and action, we shall understand why the two cannot exist in the mind together. And since the methods employed in the control of persons and things are antagonistic to those employed in the control of self, it will not be possible to develop self-mastery so long as there is the least attempt to influence others.

It may seem impossible, however, to deal with other minds, especially with younger minds, without exercising some form of influence ; but we must remember that there is a great difference between trying to control a mind and trying to instruct a mind.

To control a mind is to compel that mind to neglect its own power ; to instruct a mind is to inspire in that mind the desire to use its own power.

To train another mind in the line of right thought and action, do not try to compel that mind to think right or act right ; place before that mind ideas that will naturally produce right thought and right action. And this can be done without having the slightest desire to influence or control.

It is upon this principle that the new education is based—the education that will not simply train small minds to remember what great minds have thought, but will train all small minds to become great minds.

GREAT is the mind that can leave everybody alone, that can be friendly to those who think what he cannot accept, and that can desire with his whole heart to have everybody be free to be themselves; but it is necessary to have such a mind if we would attain mastery of self.

If we are not to influence anyone it may be a problem to know how far we may go in persuading others to examine the desirability of the good things we have found in life. There is a natural tendency among us all to wish that everybody had all the good that we have, but we frequently go too far in trying to make people accept what they cannot appreciate. From this we observe that the human race is not depraved at all, but is somewhat lacking in judgment.

The best way and the simplest way to persuade others to take advantage of the good that you may have found, is to prove in your own life that what you have found is better.

Never try to compel others to change; leave them free to change naturally and orderly because they want to; and they will want to change when they find that your change was worth while.

To inspire in others a desire to change for the better is truly noble; but this you can do only by leaving them alone, and becoming more noble yourself.

Make the most of yourself in your way, and leave everybody free to make the most of themselves in their way; they will when they find that it is better to enter the greater than to remain in the lesser; and that that is better you can prove by the way you live.

All minds want the best, and they will soon know the best when it is constantly before them as a living reality. People may not accept your theories, but if your life is better than theirs, they will soon do their utmost to live as you do.

After all, what would one have? Is it not life, the best life, the most beautiful life that we all seek?

To completely eliminate all desire to control persons and things, impress upon mind the great fact that it is not what others do, but what you, yourself do, that determines whether good or ill shall come to you.

When this fact is realized, your one desire will be to perfect your own life, thought, and action; you will find that the mastery of yourself will require all of your time and the whole of your attention, and you will interfere with others no more.

The true understanding of freedom will also help a great deal in removing the desire to interfere with others. When one finds that he cannot receive what he is not willing to give, and that so long as we deny freedom to others, others cannot give freedom to us, the relations between man and man become so clear that anyone can understand how to relate himself to the human race.

The best way, however, is to have so much faith in others that you know they will do the best they can without your telling them to do so. Such a faith may not always bring forth the best from everybody, but it will produce a strong tendency in that direction; and besides, it will make of you a superior being. You will advance constantly through such a faith, and thousands will follow your example.

To eliminate all desire to control others, however, is not the only essential; you must also eliminate all desire to control your own person. Nor is this a contradiction; to control the person you must act upon that inner power that can control the person; but it is not possible to act upon the power that is back of the person while attention is centred upon the person itself.

You cannot control the within while trying to control the without; the within is the world of cause, while the person is but the effect of what is being expressed from the inner cause.

As the subjective is, so is the objective;

the subjective is the inner life, and originates everything that appears in the objective or outer life.

We must not try to control the person, whether that person belongs to us or to some other soul.

True, we are to master the person, but we cannot master the person by concentrating attention upon the person; we master the person by expressing through the person those conditions and actions that we desire to see in the person, and those can be brought forth only from the within.

You can produce any change desired in the person by creating the cause of that change in the subconscious; and you can make the person express any desired action by creating the subconscious cause of that action. Nothing can be done, however, in the person, or through the person, unless the necessary cause is first produced in the subconscious, or what is frequently termed the subjective side of mind.

It is therefore evident that all effort to control the person or act upon the person, is wasted effort; results can be secured in the person only through that action that deals with the power back of the person, because what this power does, that the person will do also.

THE mastery of self implies the power to make the greatest and the best use of self, and to exercise this power is the real purpose of mastery; therefore, those mental states through which this power can act with the greatest efficiency must be cultivated.

The first essential mental state is harmony; complete and universal harmony, harmony with oneself, with everybody, and with everything.

To be in harmony is to be properly related to that with which we may come in contact; and to be properly related to anything is to meet that something in its own world without disregarding the purpose of our world.

To be in harmony with everything is to adapt yourself to everything, and though this is an art requiring much thought and effort, it is absolutely necessary, because when one is not in harmony he is in discord, and discord misdirects energy.

To cultivate harmony, concentrate attention frequently upon the interior principle of harmony, the soul of harmony as it exists in the ideal within.

There is a state in the within that not

only is in harmony, but that is harmony; and to mentally grow in the consciousness of that state is to unfold the life of harmony throughout one's entire personality.   EQUANIMITY

The second essential mental state is poise, and its chief value in self-mastery is the part it plays in holding together the energies of the system.

The mastery of self implies the possession of self, the conscious possession of one's entire self; that is, the holding together of the various activities, forces, and elements in the system so that they may all work in unison in promoting the purpose the mind may now have in view.   And this is poise.

Through the law of harmony you may change your mental attitudes at will, because when the consciousness of harmony is attained, you have not only the power to change your attitude so as to harmonize yourself with everything, but you also discern instantaneously when to change, and in what way.

Through the law of poise, however, you gain the power to prevent mental change, which at times, and in a certain sense is absolutely necessary.

To be ever the same and yet never the same is to be on the perfect path to the greater life.

All the energies of the system must be held together in poise even when you are changing your mental attitudes to harmonize with something that is different.

Every change demands a law through which to produce its change; but this law does not change. The law is ever the same, and yet he who applies this law will be never the same.

The attitude of poise is the changeless attitude through which all energies must pass if constructive results and change for the better are to be secured. It is therefore indispensable to the attainment of self-mastery, because to master the forces of the system is to have conscious possession of those forces, and that is poise.

To cultivate the attitude of poise, combine in consciousness the feeling of power and the feeling of peace. To feel immensely strong, and perfectly serene at the same time, is to be in poise.

The feeling of poise produces the feeling of self-possession, and to concentrate attention frequently upon our most perfect mental conception of the state of self-possession will develop the attitude of poise.

The third essential mental state is non-resistance; and the value of this state in the mastery of self is beyond measure.

To practice resistance is to direct attention upon the objective; it is trying to force things, and this causes the mind to act directly upon things; consciousness is brought to the surface, and the mental forces will begin to move towards the without instead of towards the within.

What we try to resist we try to control; and so long as we try to control anything we cannot attain the mastery of self.

The mental actions of resistance employ the external will altogether, something that must be eliminated completely before mastery can take place.

The external will, that is, ordinary will-power, is one of the principal obstacles to the attainment of self-mastery, and so long as we practice resistance this will-power will live and grow.

The stronger the power of the ordinary will, the larger will be the time required to attain the mastery of self, unless that form of will-power is eliminated completely at the beginning.

Resistance, however, is the chief promoter of this form of will-power; therefore, non-resistance must be made the one great rule in everything, whether in life, thought, or action.

To practice resistance is to try to overcome by going against; to practice non-resistance is to overcome by going above. Resistance wastes its energy by fighting what it does not want; non-resistance leaves behind what it does not want, and proceeds serenely to employ its energy in creating what it does want.

It is therefore evident that resistance never can succeed while non-resistance always does succeed.

To enter the attitude of non-resistance is not to bring your life to a standstill, nor to fold your arms, permitting persons, circumstances, and things to do to you what they like. Non-resistance is a forward movement, while resistance is never anything but retrogression.

The non-resisting mind does not antagonize the wrongs that are behind, and all wrongs are behind, but proceeds in peace to realize the greater good that is before.

The attitude of non-resistance makes man a stronger individuality, and he who becomes stronger will not remain in the hands of the weaker.

To resist what is against us is to continue to be small, and he who is small cannot overcome those obstacles that may seem to be great.

Resistance scatters and wastes energy; non-resistance accumulates and constructively employs energy. Therefore, to practice the former is to remain weak, while to practice the latter is to develop strength and power in greater and greater measure.

To use your power in resisting wrongs is to continue in bondage to those wrongs, because we give our power to that which we resist. To use your power for self-development and self-mastery is to rise superior to every circumstance and condition, which means inevitable victory and complete emancipation.

THE fourth essential mental state is receptivity, or the attitude of responsiveness—that attitude that places the mind in perfect touch with everything that it may desire to receive.

The objective or personal life is controlled by causing the objective to respond to the subjective, and there is positively no other law through which the person may be controlled.

It is not necessary to act upon the person to control the person, nor would such action produce any results whatever; the person will respond only to that which is taking place in the within ; therefore, to create the desired subjective action, and train the person to respond to that action, is to secure the desired objective action.

The mastery of the personal self depends entirely upon the degree of responsiveness that exists in the person; but how can responsiveness be cultivated in the person if we are not to act upon the person? And if this quality is developed from within, how can the person, in the beginning, respond even to responsiveness ?

The fact is that receptivity has its existence primarily in consciousness, and as consciousness fills the personal self, everything that is developed in consciousness will be active in the person.

When you become conscious of the state of receptivity, the person will respond to everything with which you may come in contact, whether the contact be with the without or with the within.

The receptive mind is easily influenced and affected by everything, both good and otherwise; for this reason, no mind should place itself in sympathetic contact with environments that are contrary to its own ideals.

What enters mind from adverse environments or inferior associations will manifest in the person according to the degree of receptivity that may be present at the time; but since it is possible to control the attitude of receptivity so that we come in mental contact only with that which is desirable, every person may determine what he is to receive, and what he is not to receive, from the physical or mental worlds in which he may be living now.

The power that environment may exercise in the life of any person depends entirely upon himself, how receptive he may happen to be; but since anyone can train himself to respond only to those things that are superior to himself, he may eliminate completely every form of influence that may come from those circumstances, persons, or things that are inferior.

It is absolutely necessary that the person should respond to the mind if it is to be mastered by the mind, but since the person, when highly receptive, will respond to everything that enters the mind, nothing that is inferior or undesirable must be permitted to enter the mind.

To prevent this, however, another, and a corresponding state of mind, viz., positiveness, must be cultivated.

The person that is not receptive is barely alive, and can accomplish nothing of real value; receptivity is, therefore, indispensable, and the fact that the receptive person responds to that which is not good, as well as to that which is good, should not cause any hesitancy in the cultivation of receptivity.

The person does not respond directly to anything that exists in the without, but only to that which has first entered the mind, and the mind has the power to select from every source what it wants to accept, and reject what it does not wish to use.

To cultivate the state of receptivity, encourage the actions of the finer forces and the finer vibrations in the system. Whenever these forces are felt, the mind should become quiet and should enter more deeply into the feeling of those forces.

It is the finer forces to which the person

responds; therefore, to promote the development of receptivity the action of these forces
should be increased perpetually through the
entire personality.

Another essential to the cultivation of
receptivity is to enter into the closest possible
mental touch with the finer elements that
permeate all things; mentally live with the
soul of things; and this is the true receptivity.

When we realize the great value of receptivity, and find that the person can respond
to the low as well as to the high, it becomes
necessary to find a method through which
this delicate faculty may be so guarded and
directed that it will respond only to the
superior.

In other words, how shall the mind protect
itself from being impressed with the many
inferior things with which we come in daily
contact?

What we see, hear, or feel, or meet in any
way, produces some impression upon the
mind; in fact, everything that enters through
the senses will impress the mind, and every
impression, if sufficiently strong, will affect
the mind, and then the person.

We cannot close our eyes to what we see;
we must, therefore, find a method through
which we may prevent what we do see from
impressing the mind when we so elect.

We want all our senses to be thoroughly
alive, and we want consciousness to be wide-

awake to everything that is taking place in our present state of existence, but we also want the power to close the mental door to every impression from without that is not worthy of being entertained.

This power is found in the state of positiveness, the fifth essential mental state.

So long as the mind is in a positive state, nothing can impress the mind unless that impression is deeply desired, and the reason why is simple.

It is the creative energies of mind that produce the mental impressions, but these energies will do only what they are directed to do by the vibrations that enter the mind. These vibrations may come from without, through the senses, or they may come from within, through the mind's own thinking, and the creative energies will obey those vibrations that have the greatest power.

When the vibrations from without are the strongest, as is the case in the average mind, the creative energies will proceed to form impressions, states, conditions, and thoughts that are exactly similar to the ideas that are being conveyed by the vibrations from without; and the mental world will be created in the likeness of the exterior environment.

However, when the mind is in a positive state, the vibrations from within are the strongest, and no vibration from without can produce an impression upon the mind unless the mental door is consciously opened to that particular idea.

When you are in a positive state, nothing that you may see, hear, or feel will impress your mind unless you so desire. It is therefore evident that so long as you remain in a positive state, you will never be controlled by environments, circumstances, persons, or things.

Positiveness is that state wherein the mind generates its own vibrations and its own mental life; forms its own mental attitudes, thinks consciously its own thoughts, and is so strong in its own individualized being that no power can act in the mental domain unless it is wanted.

To be positive, however, does not mean to domineer over anything, but to feel the fullness of invincible life and power, and to fill the mind with the fullness of that life and power.

You do not have to exercise control over the forces of the mind; you do not have to compel the creative energies to ignore the vibrations, the influences, and the ideas that come from without; it is simply necessary to fill your own mind with your own mental vibrations, and to make those vibrations stronger than those that may try to enter from without.

So long as you fill your mind with your

own mental vibrations, and you always do when in a positive state, the creative energies will produce only those thoughts and impressions that you desire to have produced; the desires of your own true self will be obeyed by the powers within you, and those desires alone.

The value of positiveness lies, first, in its power to protect the mind from being impressed by inferior, external conditions; and secondly, in its power to keep the creative energies under the complete control of the mind.

The positive mind has the power to think whatever it may want to think, and this is the real secret of the mastery of self.

He alone can master himself who can master his mind; and he alone can master his mind who can think what he wants to think, at any time and under any circumstance.

To develop positiveness, simply be positive at all times; that is the whole secret, and it is something that any one can do with perfect ease.

Feel the fullness of invincible life and power, and fill your mind with this life and power. Resist nothing, domineer over nothing, and try to control nothing. Feel positively that you are a master, because that is what you are.

The sixth essential mental state to the

attainment of the mastery of self, is the consciousness of superiority.

It is not possible to attain self-mastery so long as one thinks that he is an inferior creature, because through that thought mind goes down and functions below its true level.

We can control only that which we ·have risen above ; therefore, no mastery is possible until we live in the mental world of superiority.

The idea, however, is not that we are to think of ourselves as being superior to others ; we know that the same superiority that exists in us exists in every person, and it is this superiority into which we desire to enter.

The idea is to dwell constantly upon the mountain top of your being ; to live consciously and perpetually at the very apex of all your aspirations, and to constantly function in the most perfect spheres of those present possibilities that you can now realize.

The purpose of self-mastery is to make all of life just as high as our highest vision of the ideal ; and we have attained mastery when we can make everything in life become exactly what we wish it to be.

The act of mastering oneself implies the power to bring oneself up to the state of superiority ; to make everything superior to what it was, and then press on to still greater heights.

The purpose of mastery is not to control

faculties, talents, forces, or elements, but to direct them all towards greater attainments and greater achievements—towards superiority.

It is not possible, however, to cause everything in one's being to move towards superiority unless the mind is established in the consciousness of superiority; to produce mental tendencies towards the superior, consciousness must feel the life, the spirit, and the soul of the superior, and this feeling may be cultivated by frequently concentrating attention upon the most perfect conception of superiority that the mind can possibly form.

Whatever we frequently think of, with depth and feeling, that we shall gain the consciousness of; this is a law through which any hidden secret may be brought into the light of a clear, positive understanding.

The seventh essential mental state is the realization of supremacy; the knowing of the truth that you, yourself, are the supreme ruler over everything in your being and in your world.

We must remove the idea of exercising control over the person through the use of objective will-power, and in the place of that idea establish the realization of supremacy.

When one knows that he is the supreme master of his being, he rules supremely without trying to do so; and herein we learn why he who has attained the mastery of self never tries to master or control anything, not even himself.

It is not necessary to try to be that which you are; and as you are created with the power to master yourself, you do not have to try, at any time, to master yourself. You are the supreme master of your being, and to think the truth, you must think of yourself as such.

He *is* what he is who knows that he *is*; and he who knows *what* he is, does what he *can* do by the virtue of being what he *is*.

He who knows that he is supreme in his own being exercises supremacy by the virtue of being supreme.

He who is supreme cannot do otherwise but exercise supremacy; and since man is supreme in his own being he must necessarily exercise supremacy in his own being; that is, when he knows that he is what he *is*.

Man in the real is a master; therefore, when in the consciousness of the real, he does master; and does not have to try. He who tries to be a master does not know that he really is a master; when he knows that he is, he will do that which he has the power to do, not by trying, but by doing what he is in being.

The sun does not try to shine; it is light; therefore, it does shine. The sun does not have to control the sunbeams: the sun creates the sunbeams by being the cause of sunbeams; the sunbeams are created to give light because they proceed from that which is light; and that which is created to give light will give light because it is light; it will not have to be controlled to do so.

A piece of ice *is* cold, therefore, it makes everything cold with which it comes in contact; it does not have to try to produce cold. It is not necessary for any force or element in nature to try to produce in itself that which already exists in itself; neither is it necessary for man to try to do this.

So long as we try to master ourselves we shall not succeed in mastering anything; but when we discover that we in truth *are* masters, we shall succeed in mastering everything without trying in the least to do so.

The realization of supremacy is therefore of the highest value, because this realization will reveal man to himself. He will *know* that he is supreme in his own being; he will know that he is created with that power, and when man knows what he is he will act accordingly.

To cultivate the mental state of supremacy, impress the mind as frequently as possible with the truth that you are supreme in your own being. If you were not, you could not exist; your being would be chaos; the fact that you exist as an individualized entity proves that you are supreme in the being of that entity, and to be just to yourself you must exercise the whole of that power.

Therefore, to impress the mind with the idea that you are supreme in your being, is simply to train your mind to understand a great truth; and when that truth is realized, the realization of supremacy will have been attained; you will know what you are and you will act with supremacy in everything that is done within yourself.

When the mind acts with supremacy in the within, all the creations of mind will be patterned after the highest ideals that may now exist in consciousness; and the progress of the individual will be remarkable.

The reason why so many fail to reach their ideals is because they do not act with supremacy in the inner world of creation; they, therefore, do not recreate themselves in the likeness of their ideals, and no person can realize his ideals until he grows into the exact likeness of those ideals.

When the mind has not attained the consciousness of supremacy it cannot act with supremacy; the creative energies will, consequently, follow lower ideals, and will not do what is wanted done.

To enter fully into the consciousness of supremacy, all knowledge that reveals the unlimited possibilities of man will prove of great value, because the more deeply we can penetrate the greatness already existing within us, the more firmly we can establish the consciousness of supremacy.

To constantly feel that one is supreme in his own domain is absolutely necessary, and as this feeling would simply be the conscious expression of what is the truth, no one should hesitate for a moment to enter that attitude, and to dwell therein forever.

The person may feel weak, but that does not prove that you are weak; the weakness of the person is felt because you have failed to bring forth your own real strength.

Know that you are strong, and all weakness will disappear; know that you are supreme in your own domain, and you will rule supremely in your own domain. You will rule with supreme power because you are the individualization of supreme power.

HAVING established the mind in the seven states that are necessary to the attainment of self-mastery, the next essential is to train the will to perform its true function.

To begin, we must discard the current belief that the will was made to rule; the very opposite is its function; the true will never attempts to rule anything, but holds itself constantly in that attitude through which it can be ruled by the mind's highest conception of law, principle, and truth.

Man attains self-mastery not by trying to rule, but by permitting himself to be ruled by that which is greater than his present conception of himself.

That personality is always the most powerful that lets go of its own personal power and gives itself up completely to superior power.

He who is willing to lose the smaller life for the sake of the larger, will gain the larger; and he who is willing to lose his limited personal power for the sake of unlimited impersonal power, will gain the unlimited.

In like manner, he who disposes of the will that tries to rule, for the sake of the will that is *the* ruler, will receive the latter, which is the real will. And this is necessary, because the mastery of self cannot be attained so long as will-power is exercised in the usual way.

The true will never tries to rule; it already is the ruling power; and it never tries to gain supremacy; it already is supreme.

Since the true will already is supreme, it would be a misuse of will to try to become supreme. Through such actions an inferior imitation of the real will would be employed, and that imitation would not contain any will-power whatever, but would simply be some aimless use of superficial mental force.

What is usually termed the personal will, that is, that something that we employ when we try to rule or domineer, is not will-power in any form; the personal will is nothing but the misuse of mental forces.

In the average person the real will is never employed; what passes for will in those minds is a more or less uncertain expression of those states of consciousness that have gained some imperfect conception of the real will.

Through every mental conception of the will a temporary state of consciousness is established having a tendency to direct, and to take initial steps. This is natural, because since the will itself is the ruling power every mental conception of the will would have a tendency to rule.

Each mental conception of the will bears a slight resemblance to the will, and receives a tendency to act accordingly. Consequently, a mental conception of the will, by virtue of this slight resemblance, imitates the will with imperfect attempts to rule.

When we take initial steps, we are said to use the will, but we do not; we simply express our latest mental conception of the will; and since all such conceptions have tendencies to rule, direct, or take initial steps, initial steps, however imperfect, will accordingly be taken.

It is the truth, well-known to everybody, that the average initial step is a mistake; and it could not very well be otherwise, because it is not taken by the real will, but by an inferior imitation. It is also well known that most of our attempts at exercising the power to rule are complete failures, and lead both object and subject into confusion.

It is also the truth, easily demonstrated, that practically all the mistakes of the world come originally from the tendency of the mind to follow imitations of the will instead of the real will itself.

The ills of life are wholly due to the mistakes we make when trying to control and direct our actions by the personal will; while the great and the good things that are done are done only when the mind gives way to a superior power, and acts under the direction and inspiration of the supreme will.

The pronounced individualist may object to the idea that we are to give up to a superior power, but such objections will disappear when we realize that this superior power is our own power, and that we are simply discarding the false and the limited in order that we may take possession of the limitless and the true.

In like manner, all objections to the idea that the will must place itself in that attitude where it can be ruled by the superior, will disappear when we realize that through that attitude of the will, the will is permitted to be itself.

In order that the will may be itself, it should make no effort to rule, but should remain what it is—*the power that does rule.*

The will is properly performing its true function when it is eternally giving way to the superior; that is, the superior that is in itself, that is in man, and that is in the expression of the infinite in man.

The true function of the will is to hold the mind in such a state that the higher may find a full and free expression at all times. In other words, to keep the mind open to the perpetual influx of life and power from on high—that is what the true will is created to do; and that is sufficient; the mind that is constantly being filled with the superior, will receive everything that it may desire to receive because the superior contains everything.

Such a mind will also become what it may wish to become, because to be filled with the superior is to become superior. It will also achieve anything that may be undertaken, because there is no limit to the power from which the superior eternally proceeds.

The difference, therefore, between the real will and its man-made imitations is immense, and any one can understand that man has nothing to lose and everything to gain by eliminating the latter and giving up completely to the power of the former.

T HE purpose of the personal will is to try to compel things to do thus or so; but this is not necessary, neither can anything but undesirable results proceed from such efforts.

Things will do that which they are created to do when left to themslves; and since everything has the inherent right to be itself and itself only, we cannot try to make them do or be different without violating the law of freedom.

When we desire different things we should cause different things to be created, and not try to make things already created different from what they are. This, however, is constantly being done; the result is, we not only misplace things, but we interfere, more or less, with the natural inclinations and best motives of nearly every person with whom we come in contact.

This practice leads to the violation of the law of freedom on every hand, and since we cannot expect to receive from others what we do not wish to give to others, there can be no freedom for ourselves until we interfere with persons and things no more.

The leading purpose of the personal will is to change things in the without; to try to make over what has already been created. In brief, the ordinary will-power is simply a meddler, and is engaged principally in the work of interference, trying to prevent persons and things from being themselves.

This purpose, however, is contrary to all the laws of life, because the very first principle in life is to give everything the freedom to be what it is.

When we wish to change things we must not misplace them, but proceed to transmute them; and transmutation is brought about, not by interfering with the present external condition of things, but through the expression of superior power into the interior life of things.

When things are not as they should be, we can change them, not by trying to remake the present external condition of things, but by creating a new internal condition for things.

We remove evil, not by resistance nor by interference, but by permitting evil to be itself, which is nothing. Evil, being mere nothingness or emptiness, would never disturb us if we did not make " something " out of it.

The more we interfere with evil the more we make of evil and the more we disturb the development of the good, thus retarding the growth of the very thing that *can* remove evil.

We cannot remove evil; this the good alone can do; but we can create the good in sufficient abundance to cause all evil to disappear.

We have no time to create the good while constantly interfering with evil; and since it is the creation of the good and the good alone that can remove evil, we understand perfectly why we should not disturb the tares.

We have given ages of time to the pulling up of tares, but there are just as many tares in the world now as there ever were. Nothing has been gained; we have not removed the ills of life by constantly interfering with those ills; the method is a complete failure, and should be abandoned absolutely.

It can be demonstrated conclusively that evil invariably disappears when left to itself, to be itself, which is nothing; but to leave evil alone, the mind must give the whole of its attention to the creation of the good.

The personal will, however, cannot leave evil alone; its nature is to interfere; therefore, it must be eliminated, and the entire mind placed absolutely in the hands of Supreme Will.

When we compare, briefly, the two methods for dealing with adverse conditions, we find that the old method, the method of the personal will, through a constant interference with evil, never succeeds in eliminating evil, while the new method, through a constant creation of the good, soon eliminates all the evil there is.

Employ the new method, and evil will continue but a short time, and it is no more ; but so long as the old method is employed, evil will live and grow, with no promise of cessation whatever.

When we examine evil we find that it is a condition of emptiness or incompleteness, and can live only until the fullness and the completeness of the opposite good appears.

The harvest of tares, which we have been told not to prevent, is therefore not some future fixed time, but any time when the true life-forces of growth are made sufficiently strong to bring evil conditions to an end.

This end can be brought about by any person, in his own life, at any time, by the giving of all his power and the whole of his attention to the creation of those good things that are necessary to fill the conditions of nothingness that may exist in the world.

The harvest of tares, that is, the end of evil conditions in any personal life, can be produced at once, and complete emancipation secured now ; but the personal will must first give way to the ruling power of the real will.

To use the will for the purpose of interfering with things, as they are, not only perpetuates evil, but also prevents everything in life from being its best.

Nothing can be its best unless it is given freedom to be itself, its true and complete self; and in order that we may enter that attitude wherein we naturally give all things the freedom to be themselves, we must permit both the perfect and the imperfect to be what they are.

Our tendency to interfere with the imperfect will disappear of itself when we realize that the imperfect will not pass away until we create something better to take its place.

However, to create that something better it is necessary to attain a higher understanding of the superior, and also to bring into action the finer creative forces. The present states of mind must give place to states that have all the essentials required for the creation of the better; but this becomes possible only when the will is employed in its true function.

THE purpose of self-mastery is the attainment of superiority; to employ all the elements of being in such a way that perpetual growth becomes the principal factor in existence.

You have attained mastery of all the forces and elements of your being when you have caused all of these to work together constantly for the higher development of your entire self.

To simply make certain forces in your system obey your desires does not indicate any degree of self-mastery; in fact, every attempt to control your forces according to personal desires will pervert the will, and thus prevent the attainment of mastery. But when any force has been made constructive and constructive only, then you are the master of that force.

It is the true purpose of all forces to be constructive; they are, therefore, not in their true sphere of action until they have become permanently constructive; and he who has accomplished this has mastered the powers of his being.

To master yourself is to cause all things in yourself to enter their true sphere of action, and the very moment that the will proceeds to direct all things in being into their true spheres of action, the first step in mastership has been attained.

The will cannot direct things, however, until it has given up completely to that superior power that is the ruling power; and its direction of things into their true spheres of action consists in the placing of things in the hands of this same power.

When analyzing the true will and its true function, we find that its one and only purpose is to act upon consciousness; not to control consciousness, but to act upon consciousness.

The will was not made to act upon the body, nor upon any of the forces and elements in the body; neither was it made to act upon the mind, nor upon any of the states, the tendencies, or the desires of the mind.

The will should act upon consciousness only, and the reason why is found in the fact that everything that appears in body or mind is but the effect of conscious states.

Whatever you become conscious of, that you will express in the personality, and mind and body will become what those expressions are. The conditions of those expressions will be externalized in the personality, and the person will feel, act, and behave exactly as those expressions feel, act, and behave.

Every change that actually takes place in

consciousness will produce a corresponding change in the personality, and every step in advance that is realized in consciousness will cause the personality to advance and develop in a similar manner.

Every cause that is formed in conscious. ness will produce its own effect in the per. sonality, and as any cause desired may be produced in consciousness, any effect desired may be secured in mind or body.

There is nothing, however, except the true will that can produce causes in conscious. ness, therefore the will must be trained for this work.

In training the will for practical purposes, the mind should be centred as much as possible upon the true function of the will; the personal will should be ignored com. pletely, and no thought whatever should be given to the exercise of control over any. thing, nor should the slightest desire to rule be permitted.

To feel a desire to rule, control, antagonize, or resist, means that the true will is not recognized, and that the mind is permitting itself to be misled by inferior imitations.

The true will always moves towards the superior; it acts upon consciousness for the purpose of causing consciousness to gain a higher and a larger conception of the superior, and as these superior conceptions are realized in mind, they become patterns for thc creative energies. Superior thoughts, desires, tendencies, actions, and conditions will thereby be created throughout the entire system.

The will is created to take the initial step in everything that transpires in human existence; and since all the elements of life follow the will, it is of the highest importance that every step be a step in advance, because if it is not, the elements of life will produce the inferior; retrogression will then take place, and the very things that are not wanted will appear in life.

However, when the will is true every step that is taken will be a step in advance, a step towards the consciousness of greater superiority; the true will is superior, therefore can will to act only in the life of superiority.

The will is superior now; it is above all other functions and attributes; nothing takes place until the will acts; it is the master over all, and therefore occupies the highest place in mind. Consequently, when we recognize the will in its true state, we recognize something that is superior, and all our thoughts will ascend towards the superior.

When all the actions of mind are moving towards the superior, greatness is being developed and the purpose of mastery is being fulfilled.

We master any particular part of the

system when that part is made to perform its true function under all sorts of conditions; and we further master the same part when we have trained it to perform its function much better than it ever did before.

To cause this perfect action, and the more perfect action, to take place in any particular part of the system, this action must first be caused in consciousness, because each part of the system simply carries out what consciousness holds for it to do. The various forces, elements, organs, and states are mere channels of expression for conscious action.

Change a certain phase of consciousness, and the corresponding mental or physical expression changes likewise; but no change can possibly take place in any part of the personality until the necessary change is produced in consciousness; and nothing can produce this change in consciousness but the true action of the true will.

The prevailing state of consciousness is the only one cause in the personal being of man; all other things are effects of this one cause; it is therefore useless for the will to act upon anything else but consciousness, because it is only through consciousness that the purpose of the will can be promoted.

To train the will to will in harmony with the real will, form in mind a clear conception of the real will; then will only the larger, the higher, and the better.

As the consciousness of the real will is developed, the will-power becomes immensely strong; and there are two reasons why; first, because the true will does not destroy its strength through the desire to rule; and second, because it gives itself up to the influx of real power—the power that proceeds from the source of limitless power.

As this power fills the system more and more, a deep stillness is gained, a state of being that is not only perfectly serene, but immensely strong; peace and power united; and when this state of being is felt, one may know that the path to self-mastery has been found.

To enter this state is to begin the mastery of self, and to continue in this state is to continue to develop the mastery of self to the very highest possible degree.

To step outside of this state is to cease, for the time being, to master oneself, and herein one may know whether he is on the path to mastery or not.

To hold the mind and every part of the mind in this serene, strong state, and to hold it there at all times, is a very high art, and is made possible only through the training of the will to act upon the principle of the real will.

When the will wills to be what it *is*—the

ruling power, and wills to feel the action of this power, the mind will enter the strong, serene state, because the action of the real will is perfectly serene, and its power is immensely strong.

TO MASTER oneself is to cause oneself to be what one wishes to be. To eternally become what one desires to become means a perpetual transformation of self because all becoming is change —eternal change for the better; and to perpetually transform the self, a higher order of life and thought must be constantly expressed in the self.

This, however, is made possible only through awakening of higher and larger states of consciousness, and as consciousness responds only to the actions of the will, the true use of the will becomes indispensable in the attainment of the mastery of self.

To train the will to act upon consciousness, will-power should be concentrated upon every individualization of consciousness in the personality as well as upon consciousness in general.

If we wish to produce a certain effect in any part of the personality, the will should act upon the consciousness that permeates that part, and the cause that can produce the desired effect should be impressed upon that state of consciousness.

Consciousness permeates every atom in your entire being, and every atom responds to the action of that part of consciousness that is centred within the atom; it is there-fore possible to produce any desired phy-sical or chemical effect in any part of the personality by producing in the conscious-ness within that part the desired cause.

There is a special centre of consciousness in every organ of the body, and in every faculty of the mind; therefore, to produce any desired effect upon any special organ or faculty, the will must act, not upon the organ or faculty itself, but upon the centre of con-sciousness that is within that organ or faculty.

The reason why the average person fails to control his body or mind is because he uses will-power upon the body and the mind instead of upon the consciousness that permeates both.

Control the consciousness that permeates the body and you control the body as well; and consciousness is readily controlled when the will acts directly upon consciousness while strongly desiring to secure certain results.

To cause the will to act directly upon consciousness, concentrate attention upon the finest substance or life that you can picture as permeating that part of mind or body where you desire the effect to be produced.

To illustrate, when concentrating upon the

brain do not think of the brain itself, nor use will-power upon the brain, but turn will and attention upon the finer life-forces that permeate the brain. Likewise when concentrating upon any organ in the body, do not direct the will upon the physical organ, but upon the finer forces that permeate that organ. In this way you will act directly upon the centre of consciousness within that organ, and whatever you impress that centre of consciousness to do, the organ itself will do.

Through the same process the centre of consciousness in any organ or faculty may be so strongly individualized that it will respond instantaneously to any action that may be made by the will. The stronger the centre of consciousness in any part of the personality the stronger the subconscious action of the will in that centre; and as it is the subconscious action of the will that controls, the value of developing strong centres of consciousness in every part of the personality becomes evident.

When attention is being concentrated upon the various centres of consciousness, the will must never try to control those centres, or domineer, in any way, over consciousness itself. The object of the will is to impress upon consciousness those actions or qualities that are desired in personal expression.

To promote this object, the force of will and the force of desire should be combined into one action, and this action should be directed where results are to be secured.

The true will and the true desire are the two halves of the same whole; they are therefore indispensable to each other, and the more thoroughly they are trained to work as one, the sooner will the mastery of self be attained.

Desire receives, and the will directs action upon the object that the mind wishes to receive. Before the mind can receive, consciousness must come in contact with the object desired, and to direct consciousness into that contact, the will is required, because the will is the only power that can direct.

When desire acts without the will, it fails to bring consciousness into contact with the object desired; nothing is therefore received; and this explains why most desires are never fulfilled.

When the will acts without desire, the mental attitude that receives and appropriates is absent; there is no receptivity, therefore, nothing is received; and this explains why mere will-power is powerless to gain the object in view.

When the will acts upon a certain state of consciousness, there should be a very strong desire to awaken into positive action what may be latent in that state; and, conversely, whenever the mind feels a strong desire for something, the will should act directly upon the inner or subjective state of that centre of consciousness that contains that something.

Through these methods, what we desire to receive will be received, and what we will to accomplish will be accomplished.

The desire that is aimless, and the will that domineers but never directs—these two actions in mind are responsible for nearly all the failures in life; it is therefore evident that failure could be reduced to a minimum in every sphere of life when the force of desire and the force of will were combined into one perfect action.

Such an action would be irresistible, and would invariably gain what it willed and desired to gain. It would be the action of complete mastery wherever it willed and desired to act.

We may desire power for ages, but so long as consciousness is not placed in touch with the inner source of power, we shall desire in vain. We can receive nothing from any source, until we place mind in contact with that source, and to produce that contact, the will must direct consciousness to become conscious of that source.

It is the truth that we may gain possession of anything in the external world that we may require, if we unfold the necessary capacity and ability from the internal world; but again, it is only the true use of the will, combined with a strong desire, that can place mind in touch with the limitless power of this internal ability.

To use will-power without desire is to stupify the mind; and here we have one reason why so many minds lack brilliancy.

To use desire without will is to place the mind in a negative state, where it may be controlled by anything that may appear in its environment.

To combine the force of will and the force of desire into one action no particular method is required, except to will to desire whatever you desire to desire, and to desire to accomplish whatever you will to accomplish.

Whenever you desire to unfold and express a certain condition, state, or quality in your being, cause the will to act upon the inner consciousness of that condition, state, or quality; and when you employ the will in any way whatever, desire something definite at the time, with the very strongest desire that you can possibly arouse.

When causing the will to act upon consciousness, think of the soul of things; consciousness is always reached when attention is concentrated upon the *soul* of things, because consciousness is that finer something that permeates the soul of things. It has neither shape nor form, yet it is *in* all shapes and forms.

WHAT is termed the soul of things is the inner world of limitless possibility; therefore, by causing will and desire to act upon the inner world of consciousness, the greater things that are latent within are unfolded, developed, and expressed.

We thereby train ourselves to promote the purpose of self-mastery to a greater and a greater degree, because we attain the mastery of self only by eternally bringing forth a superior self.

It is therefore evident that every attempt towards self-mastery must have the superior self always in view; and this is accomplished perfectly when the forces of will and desire act invariably upon the inner consciousness of everything in the human system.

When the self is perfect, as far as its present requirements are concerned, it needs no control; it will be right and do right because it is right. When a certain organ in the body performs its function perfectly, it needs no attention; it needs no control in order that it may do its work; it is already subconsciously controlled by its own state of harmony with the real will.

It is the same with everything in the system; no mastery is needed over anything while it is doing its work perfectly, because it is already in the hands of mastery; but if it is not doing its work perfectly, it needs transformation, not control.

You cannot control the wrong to be right; but you can transmute and transform the wrong into the right; you can gradually transform the inferior into the superior, and it has been demonstrated that when the entire system is being steadily transformed, every part of the system will not only perform its function properly, but will perpetually improve the work of that function.

The best way to keep the entire system in order, is to constantly improve the entire system; and this is the purpose of self-mastery.

To master self is not to try to control self, but to perpetually transform self; it means continuous advancement for every part of the being of man; it is the elimination of evil through a constant growth in the realization of the good; it is overcoming the imperfect by creating the perfect; it is the passing out of the lesser through the passing into the greater; it is the prevention of retrogression through the perpetual promotion of progression.

The law of continuous advancement, however, is based upon the principle that every change or improvement that is to be produced in life must come from the unfoldment of the greater possibilities that are latent in life. We advance in the without by unfolding and expressing the greater from the within; and we master the self by causing the self to eternally become what is latent in the superior life within the self.

The mastery of self may therefore be promoted only through the practical application of this principle; that is, every action of mind, desire, or will must act upon the greater within. Before a desired effect can be secured in the without, the corresponding cause must be created in the within; and to create this cause, action must be concentrated upon the consciousness of the within.

To control the forces of the system, the mind, through the united action of will and desire, must act upon the finer forces that permeate the finer elements throughout the system. Produce any desired impression upon the finer forces while mentally entering into the inner world of the finer forces, and the outer forces of the personality will act exactly as the impression desired.

Discord, confusion, irritability, restlessness, or pain among the forces of the system can be removed instantaneously by impressing upon the finer forces the desire for peace, serenity, harmony, and poise.

When the mind enters the finer forces

while in the attitude of harmony, perfect harmony will immediately be established throughout the personality.

This is how adverse conditions in the system may be mastered; not by trying to control those conditions, but by entering into the finer consciousness and creating there more perfect conditions.

Whenever you wish to change physical action, direct attention upon the subjective side, that is, the finer consciousness that permeates that part of the physical form through which the new action is to appear, and desire that subjective side to act the way you wish the physical part to act; and as soon as the desired subjective action is produced the corresponding physical action will immediately follow.

In this way, the body can be controlled completely, and caused to act in any way that we may desire.

To remove physical pain or disease, concentrate attention upon the finer consciousness of that part of the body where the pain is felt. Do not think of the body itself, nor the ailment, but cause the mind to enter into the finer elements and the finer forces that permeate that part of the body where the adverse condition appears.

While in the attitude of concentration, use the will in drawing all the forces of that part of the body into the finer vibrations, and desire, with deep feeling, to realize the health and the wholeness of this finer life into which the mind has entered.

The reaction will soon follow, and the adverse condition will be caused to disappear by the coming forth of a strong, wholesome life from within.

Every unpleasant sensation in the physical system can be removed by refining the vibrations in those parts where the sensations are felt; and the vibrations of any part of the system will be refined when attention is concentrated upon the finer forces that permeate those parts.

To master your mental attitudes, turn attention upon the silent within. There is a state in the inner field of consciousness where absolute peace prevails at all times; to become conscious of this state is to become calm and serene, and by directing attention upon this state the realization of peace will immediately follow.

When in the midst of confusion, do not permit your mental forces to run towards the surface; to do this is to become confused, and thus be controlled by the confusion that exists about you.

Draw all your mental forces towards the within, while in such surroundings, and think towards the peaceful within; you will thereby realize peace, and be in peace. You will master yourself in the midst of the

storm; you will remain untouched, un-
moved, and undisturbed.

To control your thoughts, do not try
to control those thoughts that you are
thinking now, but use the will in producing
a new line of thinking. If the will is well
trained this can be done at once, and as
the mind becomes active in new fields of
consciousness, those thoughts that we did
not wish to entertain will disappear of
themselves.

To think of something different becomes
simplicity itself when the mind enters into
the finer consciousness of new thought. It
is only when the mind continues to act upon
the surface that it is difficult to change the
mind.

To control your feelings, enter into the
finer feeling of the opposite states of feeling.
Having decided upon the way you want to
feel, turn attention upon the finer consciousness of the state of feeling desired. The
desired state will soon be felt in every part of
the system.

To control desires, transmute the forces
that are trying to express themselves through
those desires; then turn the transmuted
energy into those parts of mind or body
where expression may legitimately take
place now.

To transmute the energies that are alive
in any desire, concentrate attention upon

that part of mind or body where the desire is centralized, and with the action of desire and will draw all the finer forces of that part towards the subjective side.

When the finer forces are felt, attention may be turned upon any part of the body or into any faculty where added power can be used with profit. Wherever attention is directed, there the finer forces will accumulate, that is, when the consciousness of those forces has been attained.

Through this same process all the finer elements and forces in the personality or the mentality may be called into action, and superior results secured in everything one may undertake to do.

All the forces of the system are creative, and the creative process may be promoted anywhere in the system by any of the forces of the system; therefore, if the creative function cannot now take place in the personality, the same force may be employed now in any part of the mentality. This being true, it is wasted effort to try to subdue one's physical passions; when physical desires are felt, and it is not possible to express them physically at the time, the force of those desires should be transmuted, and concentrated upon some mental creative process.

To apply the principle of self-mastery to the moral nature, the true method is, not to say no to the wrong, but to say yes to the right.

To control yourself in the midst of temptation, divert your attention from those things that you do not want, and cause the will to act upon the inner consciousness of those qualities and virtues that you do want.

To resist temptation is to fix attention upon the very thing that you do not wish to do; the mind will think more and more of the wrong until it becomes oblivious to the right, and will consequently do what it was tempted to do.

To concentrate the whole of attention upon the wrong is to cause all the tendencies of mind to move towards the wrong; the mind will think the wrong and be placed in bondage to the wrong; it will follow the wrong and act accordingly.

The secret of overcoming temptation is to refuse to give the wrong step a single moment of attention; do not resist it; do not even think about it, but give the whole of attention to the right step.

This will not be difficult if the mind, when concentrating upon the right step, will look within and view the superior side of the right step; because when its superiority is discerned, the interest in the right step will become so great that nothing could persuade the mind to think of anything else.

The various mental states of depression,

gloom, despondency, worry, etc., are produced by the mind coming down to inferior planes of action. To control those states, that is, to remove them completely, turn all the forces of mind upon the highest state of consciousness that the imagination can picture. Then direct the will to act upon the finer consciousness of this state, and into the finer state the entire mind will go.

No attempt should be made to control the temper; this will simply place the mind more completely in bondage to the forces of temper. It will also give life and power to the present personal will.

When a person becomes angry he throws his thoughts out towards the object of his ill-will, thereby bringing consciousness to the surface, away from the real will and into the personal will. His energies are wasted, poise is lost, and practically all the actions of mind are misdirected; to try to control anything while in such a state would, therefore, be useless.

To avoid becoming angry under every circumstance, do not permit the actions of the mind to move outwardly against anything when antagonized, but direct all the forces of mind inwardly at once. This will prevent the antagonistic attitude, and so long as there is no antagonistic attitude there will be no feeling of anger.

To prevent thoughts from going out when

provocations appear, impress daily upon mind the most perfect conception of a wholesome nature that can be formed, and train all the tendencies of mind to focus upon this ideal.

This will not only cause the creative energies of mind to build a sweet and wholesome nature, but the tendency of all feelings and emotions to move towards this inner ideal will become so strong that nothing can cause the force of feeling to go out against anything.

When this state has been established, all temper has been mastered, because all those forces that were previously wasted in temper have been turned in their courses, and are now engaged in the development of kindness, sympathy, tenderness, and love.

To master anything is to turn it to better use; and all things are turned to better use that are trained to work in harmony with the law of continuous advancement.

To control circumstances, the principle is to establish in yourself what you wish your circumstances to be. The mind that has created the ideal mental world will gravitate, through absolute law, into an ideal physical world.

However, before man can create an ideal internal world he must attain that state of self-possession where he will not be influenced by the adverse in the external world.

He must control himself in the midst of circumstances before circumstances will respond to his control.

In the midst of adverse circumstances, it is your thought and feeling that must be controlled, and to control thought under such circumstances all thought must be given to the ideal circumstance that you have in view.

To meet and overcome adversity it must be approached, not as an enemy, but as a force that can be turned to a better use. Adversity is but misdirected energy; but if you remain calm and strong, it will follow you, and do what you may desire to have done.

When you become stronger in your own conscious being than the forces that are about you, those forces will obey your will. For this reason, he who has mastered himself has mastered the universe.

The forces about you will not obey your will when you try to control them; they will follow you and obey you only when you have become stronger than they.

Circumstances do not have to be controlled; when the forces that are active in our circumstances are used intelligently, which means constructively, those circumstances will be in our hands without our trying to place them there.

It is necessary, however, to be calm and

self-possessed in order to use those forces intelligently; therefore, the principal essential in the midst of circumstances is to control the mode of thinking. He who can do this can turn everything to good account that may enter his path.

There is only one mode of thinking that is conducive to self-mastery, and that is scientific thinking; therefore, to control thinking is to think scientifically.

To think scientifically is to cause all the forces of mind to work together for the object that one has in view; and when all the forces of mind work for this object, the forces of circumstance will work for the same object; that is, if the force of mind is stronger than the force of circumstance.

Every person that thinks scientifically, and that unites all his forces upon the one object in view, will be stronger than his circumstances, and will thereby control those circumstances absolutely.

In the last analysis, therefore, the control of everything depends upon the control of self, and must necessarily follow the control of self; but he who would control himself must not try to control himself; he must not try to control anything; in brief, he must eliminate completely every desire that desires to exercise the power to rule. Instead, he must place himself absolutely in the consciousness of that power within that does rule—the power that is supreme.

He who gives himself to supreme power, will give expression to his own supreme power; and the expression of supreme power through every part of the self constitutes the mastery of self.

COSIMO is a specialty publisher of books and publications that inspire, inform and engage readers. Our mission is to offer unique books to niche audiences around the world.

COSIMO CLASSICS offers a collection of distinctive titles by the great authors and thinkers throughout the ages. At **COSIMO CLASSICS** timeless classics find a new life as affordable books, covering a variety of subjects including: *Biographies, Business, History, Mythology, Personal Development, Philosophy, Religion and Spirituality,* and much more!

COSIMO-on-DEMAND publishes books and publications for innovative authors, non-profit organizations and businesses. **COSIMO-on-DEMAND** specializes in bringing books back into print, publishing new books quickly and effectively, and making these publications available to readers around the world.

COSIMO REPORTS publishes public reports that affect your world: from global trends to the economy, and from health to geo-politics.

Printed in the United States
149308LV00001B/34/A

9 781602 061767